Classic cocktails from around the world

Classic cocktails from around the world

Allan Gage

hamlyn

For Jeff and Judi, the happiest couple I know...

First published in Great Britain in 2004 by
Hamlyn, a division of Octopus Publishing Group Ltd
2–4 Heron Quays, London E14 4JP

First published in paperback in 2006

Distributed in the United States and Canada by
Sterling Publishing Co., Inc.
387 Park Avenue South, New York, NY 10016-8810

This material was previously published as *Around the
World in 80 Bars*

ISBN-13: 978-0-600-61543-9
ISBN-10: 0-600-61543-X

A CIP catalogue record for this book is available from the
British Library

Printed and bound in China

10 9 8 7 6 5 4 3 2

CONTENTS

From the inner-city basement bars and the lobby bars of great hotels, to the sun-drenched beach bars in tropical paradises all over the world, no two bars are the same. Yet they all serve the same purpose, providing a welcoming environment in which guests can enjoy liquid refreshment. But where and when did bar culture begin?

The origin of today's typical urban cocktail lounge goes back to America's jazz age, ironically a time when the manufacture, sale and consumption of alcohol was made illegal during Prohibition. It is generally accepted that this period was when cocktail culture defined itself. Although, many of the classic cocktails were invented long before.

The early classics

Some popular classics were created well before the term 'cocktail' was coined. Among these early concoctions is the Manhattan, undisputedly invented at the Manhattan Club around 1874 at the request of Winston Churchill's American mother, Lady Randolph Churchill. The Cuba Libre (literally meaning 'free Cuba') was created at the end of the Spanish-American War of 1886, following the invention of Coca Cola.

The Martini was first mixed in the form we recognize today at the turn of the last century; there are many claims as to who invented it. The legendary 'Professor' Jerry Thomas renamed his Gin Cocktail the Martinez back in 1887 and it is this that is most likely the Martini's ancestor. So although the mixing of drinks began in the 19th century, the term 'cocktail' was not in common use until the days of Prohibition.

A cock's tail or cock's ale?

The word 'cocktail' itself is shrouded in mystery and a number of tall tales exist. Some say it became a code word in the 'speakeasies' for a stiff drink, others that the term came from a peacock's tail, used to decorate drinks in the early 1920s. Or it may have come from Cock's Ale, a drink popularly served in colonial times during cock fights. This was a barrel of ale into which a sack of parboiled chicken, raisins, mace and brown sugar was placed and left to ferment for nine days.

It is impossible to prove the origin of this great word, but it is generally accepted that it is the generic word now used to describe mixed alcoholic drinks. Non-alcoholic cocktails are often known as mocktails.

The Prohibition years

Americans, sick of the 'ridiculous drought' as it became known, set up an entire black market of illegal drinkeries, known as 'speakeasies'.

Because the manufacture of alcohol, as well as its consumption, was made illegal during this time, spirits were predominantly distilled at home and therefore of very low quality. 'Hooch', 'Moonshine' and 'Bath-tub Gin' became common expressions. It was the rawness of these spirits that lead to the habit of mixing, more out of necessity to mask the taste than the desire to create new cocktails.

These speakeasies were often run by the figureheads of organized crime and were luxuriously decorated and frequented by society's more affluent crowd, as well as the police and lawmen whose silence was bought with drinks, showgirls and dollars.

The emergence of bar culture

Prohibition was an important period in history that proved to be a catalyst for the globalization of bar culture. Americans began crossing the Atlantic to set up bar operations in the glamorous cities of London, Paris, Rome, Venice and Madrid. They brought with them the desire to mix drinks, but now they also had the benefit of high-quality commercially produced spirits and liqueurs.

Bartenders started to invent and create cocktails similar to those we see in today's cocktail bars. Names like Bloody Mary (invented at Harry's Bar in Paris), Bellini (invented at the unrelated Harry's in Venice) and White Lady (American Bar, Savoy) began to appear, sparking a rampage of creativity never before seen behind European bars. In 1930, Harry Craddock, Head Bartender at the American Bar in the Savoy Hotel, first published the *Savoy Cocktail Book* – a wonderful collection of contemporary cocktails, illustrated in a quirky, Art Deco style. Harry's book standardized many recipes, so that a level of consistency was now achievable across the industry. Bar culture grew as entrepreneurs recognized the untapped potential of the discerning drinker.

The Great Depression

For years after Prohibition was repealed, and throughout the Depression, the bar business became stagnant. Seen as an unnecessary luxury, alcohol was strictly for the rich, famous and powerful. In 1933, the drought came to an end when the US government, realizing the vast revenues that were going untaxed, decided to catch a slice of the action. This meant a huge cleaning-up operation of the underground bar scene all over America, pushing the culture further and further afield, with Asia and Australia being firmly established as destinations for the international bar-fly.

Sun, fun and rum

The beach bar concept began in the South-eastern states of the US soon after prohibition ended, and quickly jumped to the Caribbean where holiday makers would spend hard-earned dollars in these glorious surroundings, all year round. Many of the Caribbean islands were still colonized by Western nations and saw an influx of money from their ruler's governments with which to set up luxury resorts.

Staffed by locals, these resorts would use regional produce and spirits to maintain an authentic local vibe. Rum has always been

1: flute **2:** coupette **3:** highball **4:** hurricane **5:** martini
6: rocks **7:** sling

synonymous with beach bars – rum cocktails, like the Piña Colada and the Zombie, characterize the laid-back, worry-free existence so ingrained in island life. This has now been translated to the most exotic and far-flung beaches and islands of the world. The Seychelles, the Maldives, Mauritius, Hawaii – all exhibit the same delightful mixture of blue sky, sea, sun, rum and fun....

Recent trends

Cocktails have been in and out of fashion since their golden age between the World Wars. During the Great Depression they were seen as unnecessarily flamboyant, before enjoying popularity again throughout the experimental 1960s and the hedonistic 1970s. The 1980s favoured discreet wine bars over cocktails, until Tom Cruise starred in the box-office smash 'Cocktail', popularizing a whole new method of bartending – flair. A hybrid of barmanship and circus skills, flair brought an element of theatre to an establishment and enjoyed huge popularity throughout the 1990s in the big, corporate, city bars. Its popularity has since waned and it is now considered passé exhibitionism rather than skilled showmanship.

Another element that helped to revive the cocktail industry was the invention of the Cosmopolitan by Dale de Groff, Head Bartender at the Rainbow Room in New York. The Cosmopolitan was the first 'Neo-tini'. These drinks resemble the classic Martini not by taste, but purely by the glass they are served in. Many argue this is all wrong, but nowadays there is an infinite number of new 'Martinis' being concocted and served in bars all over the world, many being named after the bar where they were invented.

The recipe for success

What really sets great bars apart are two major factors: service and mixology. Wonderful drinks can be served in a mediocre way and the experience will not be remembered fondly. However, an average drink served with courtesy, efficiency and a sense of humour will be. The ancient and often neglected art of good conversation is also crucial to a bartender's talents; it is also what makes the job enjoyable and ultimately earns the money (no one ever made a living from a bartender's basic wage).

As for mixology: this is the art of cocktail creation and requires a knack for developing and presenting concoctions that appeal to a drinking audience. The process involves taking a base spirit, adding complementary flavours, and balancing the concoction with citrus or sugar-based ingredients. Commonly used ingredients are fresh fruit, fruit purées, flavoured syrups, herbs and spices, although the list is endless and often bordering on the bizarre – saffron, thyme, honey and even quails' eggs have made appearances in some rather more adventurous drinks.

The cocktail list

Any bar will have its own cocktail list. The bar team, usually with the final approval of the Bar Manager, will develop a bespoke list for their establishment. Much like a wine list or a food menu, the cocktail list is influenced by what ingredients are available and the nature of the local palate. For example, the dimly lit basement bars of London's Soho will never sell a huge number of creamy cocktails, just as a beach bar in the Bahamas would be misguided in putting a Manhattan on its menu, given its sun-worshipping clientele.

The appearance of bar 'genres' – urban, lounge, beach, classic – has given rise to equivalent cocktail groups, which although not very clearly defined, provide the parameters for creating new and interesting cocktails. Barmen are constantly improving existing recipes, even occasionally blurring the distinction between food and drink. And while their creations may occasionally prove challenging, they are always inspirational.

Europe
1. **American Bar at The Savoy** London, England
2. **Oloroso** Edinburgh, Scotland
3. **Apartment** Belfast, Northern Ireland
4. **Ice at the Four Seasons Hotel** Dublin, Republic of Ireland
5. **Supper Club** Amsterdam, The Netherlands
6. **Archiduc** Brussels, Belgium
7. **Harry's New York Bar** Paris, France
8. **Le Loft** Cannes, France
9. **Zebra Square** Monte Carlo, Monaco
10. **Boadas** Barcelona, Spain
11. **Chicote** Madrid, Spain
12. **Bora Bora** Ibiza, Spain
13. **Crystal Bar** Rome, Italy
14. **Harry's Bar** Venice, Italy
15. **Cosmos** Athens, Greece
16. **Laila** Istanbul, Turkey
17. **Dos Piranhas** Berlin, Germany
18. **Bugsy's** Prague, Czech Republic
19. **Most** Moscow, Russia
20. **Odeon** Oslo, Norway
21. **Café Opera** Stockholm, Sweden
22. **Absolut Ice Bar** Jukkasjarvi, Sweden

Africa
23. **Eclipse** Cape Town, South Africa
24. **Baraza** Cape Town, South Africa
25. **Moyo** Johannesburg, South Africa
26. **Coconut Willy's** Mombasa, Kenya
27. **Mangapwani Beach Club** Zanzibar, Tanzania
28. **The Carnivore** Nairobi, Kenya
29. **Calabash Bar** Lagos, Nigeria
30. **The Golf Club Bar** Poste de Flacq, Mauritius
31. **La Bodega** Cairo, Egypt

Asia
32. **Indigo** Mumbai, India
33. **Solypse Café** Goa, India
34. **Naiboli Bar at the Banyan Tree** Vabbinfaru, Maldives
35. **The Glamour Bar** Shanghai, China
36. **Aria Bar** Beijing, China
37. **Montoak** Tokyo, Japan
38. **Dragon-i** Hong Kong, China
39. **Bed Supper Club** Bangkok, Thailand
40. **Rasta Baby** Koh Samui, Thailand
41. **The Long Bar** Singapore City, Singapore
42. **Mafia Bar** Seoul, South Korea
43. **Jati Bar** Bali, Indonesia

Australasia
44. **Hemmesphere** Sydney, Australia
45. **Mink** Melbourne, Australia
46. **Geisha Bar** Perth, Australia
47. **Coast** Auckland, New Zealand
48. **Bardeaux** Queenstown, New Zealand
*49. **Beachcomber Sand Bar** Mamanuca, Fiji

South + Central America
50. **Baretto** São Paulo, Brazil
51. **Garota de Ipanema** Rio de Janeiro, Brazil
52. **Maury Bar** Lima, Peru
53. **Hotel Explora** San Pedro de Atacama, Chile
54. **Mundo Bizarro** Buenos Aires, Argentina
55. **Monoloco** Antigua, Guatemala
56. **La Capilla** Tequila, Mexico
57. **Cosmo** Mexico City, Mexico

Caribbean
58. **Foxy's Tamarind Bar** Jost van Dyke, British Virgin Islands
59. **Le Select** Gustavia, St Barths
60. **After Dark** Christchurch, Barbados
61. **Ricks's Café** Westmorland, Jamaica
62. **El Floridita** Havana, Cuba
63. **La Bodeguita del Medio** Havana, Cuba
64. **Basil's Bar** Mustique, The Grenadines
65. **Miss Emily's Blue Bee Bar** Green Turtle Cay, Bahamas

North America
66. **Elbo Room** Fort Lauderdale, USA
67. **Nikki Beach Bar** Miami, USA
68. **Sky Bar** Los Angeles, USA
69. **Bemelmans Bar** New York, USA
70. **Milk and Honey** New York, USA
71. **Tonic** Boston, USA
72. **Green Mill Cocktail Lounge** Chicago, USA
73. **Zig Zag Café** Seattle, USA
74. **Tommy's** San Francisco, USA
75. **Crush Champagne Lounge** Vancouver, Canada
76. **A GoGo Lounge** Montreal, Canada
77. **Beach Club** Las Vegas, USA
78. **West** Toronto, Canada
79. **Marmont** Philadelphia, USA
*80. **Tiki Bar** West Maui, USA

* not shown on map

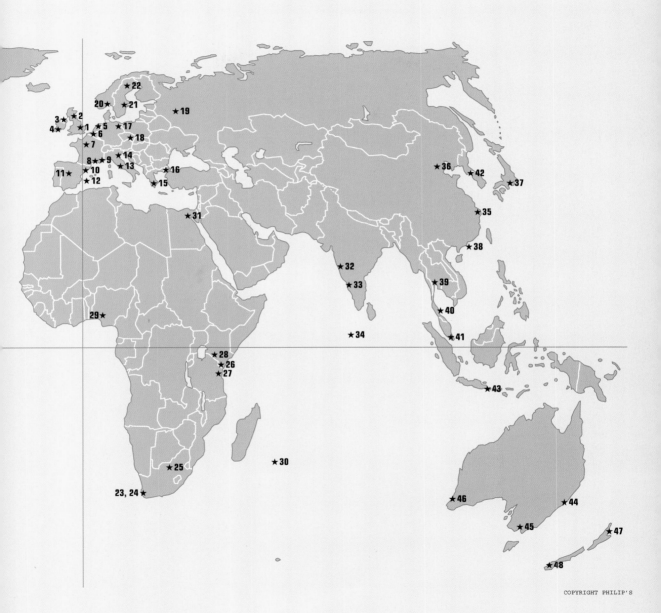

COPYRIGHT PHILIP'S

EUROPE

ENGLAND

American Bar at The Savoy *London*

A classic bar in every sense, the American Bar at The Savoy is one of London's most venerated drinking establishments. Opened in the 1930s, the bar was run by world-renowned Harry Craddock while Prohibition was in force in the US. Harry almost single-handedly sparked London's romance with cocktails and began devising magnificent bespoke recipes for special occasions, a popular tradition that continues to this day. Craddock's most famous creation was the White Lady cocktail, characterized by complex botanical flavours set against a rich, zesty backdrop and a lingering orange finish.

White Lady

1 measure gin

1 measure Cointreau

1 measure lemon juice

Pour the ingredients into a cocktail shaker. Shake and strain into a chilled Martini glass with a twist of lemon.

Oloroso *Edinburgh*

Secreted within the historic Basil Spence building, this handsome eating and drinking establishment has an expansive roof terrace that offers spectacular views of Edinburgh Castle and the Firth of Forth all year round, while the lounge has a panoramic view over the extinct volcano of Arthur's Seat. Oloroso has one of the most original cocktail lists in the country, with an imaginative menu and exemplary service at all levels. Add to this the luxurious, comfortable interiors and a unique location, and you have the ideal bar.

Red Rum

small handful of redcurrants
½ measure sloe gin
2 measures Bacardi 8-year-old rum
½ measure lemon juice
½ measure vanilla syrup

Muddle the currants and sloe gin together in the bottom of a cocktail shaker. Add the remaining ingredients with some ice cubes, shake, then double strain into a chilled Martini glass. Decorate with a string of redcurrants.

Apartment *Belfast*

'Premium product, premium service, premium experience.' True to its word, Apartment morphs from a lively morning coffee hang-out, to a bustling lunch venue, to the first cocktail bar in Northern Ireland. With a cocktail list that is constantly reviewed and ever-evolving, it remains the best bar in Belfast. Apartment launched an industry growth spurt that has led to a flourishing bar scene in Belfast, making it a genuine rival to Dublin.

Abbey Road

6 mint leaves

1 piece candied ginger

½ measure fresh lemon juice

2 measures gin

1 measure apple juice

Muddle the mint leaves, ginger and lemon juice in a cocktail shaker. Add the gin and apple juice with ice and shake. Strain over crushed ice in a rocks glass and garnish with a lemon wedge.

Ice at the Four Seasons Hotel *Dublin*

Ice is the benchmark for the flourishing cocktail culture in Dublin. The restrained décor of this hotel bar uses subtle lighting and locally commissioned art to great effect, while the bar itself stocks a superb selection of vodkas, including some delicious home-made infusions. Although the cocktail menu boasts 104 recipes at the last count, it is the original vodka creations, made with considerable skill and a healthy dose of Irish cheek, that steal the show at Ice. Hardly surprising, then, that the bar was the venue for the official launch of the prestigious Irish Film & Television Awards in 2003.

Razzmopolitan

1½ measures Stoli Razberi

1 measure Cointreau

dash of lime juice

1 measure cranberry juice

4 raspberries

Place all the ingredients in a cocktail shaker. Shake and double strain into a chilled Martini glass and decorate with 2 extra raspberries on a cocktail stick.

Supper Club *Amsterdam*

An unusual evening awaits through the doors of the Supper Club. Amidst the dazzling white décor, patrons lounge on beds lined with cushions while exquisite food and drinks are delivered to their tables. The entertainment is also truly eccentric – it might be a singer delivering an operatic aria, a mad magician or even a sculptor. The brainchild of chef and visual artist Thorwald Voss, the Supper Club has a magnificent drinks list compiled by the Fabulous Shaker Boys. Expect a delicious assault on every one of your senses.

Hong Kong Sling

1½ measures gin
½ measure lychee liqueur
1 measure lychee purée
1 measure lemon juice
½ measure sugar syrup
soda, to top up

Place all the ingredients in a cocktail shaker with ice. Shake and strain over ice into a sling glass. Stir and top up with soda. Serve with long straws and a lychee in its shell.

Expect a **delicious**
assault on every one
of your **senses**

Archiduc *Brussels*

Jazz pianist Stan Brenners opened Archiduc in the 1940s and its name remains synonymous with music. Miles Davis, the legendary trumpeter, jammed there regularly in the 1980s and Europe's finest musicians continue to play there today. As with an old Prohibition speakeasy, you ring the bell for admission. Once inside you see the Cotton Club in miniature: Art Deco styling, a half-moon mezzanine and leather bucket seats. There is no cocktail list; the staff will ask you a few key questions – long or short, sweet or sour, spirit preference – and then create something bespoke and invariably delicious.

Orange Blossom

4 slices of orange

2 teaspoons almond syrup

2 measures gin

1 measure pink grapefruit juice

3 dashes of Angostura bitters

Muddle the orange slices and syrup in the base of a highball glass. Fill the glass with crushed ice and pour in the gin. Stir, top with the grapefruit juice and bitters and garnish with extra slices of orange. Serve with straws.

FRANCE

Harry's New York Bar *Paris*

In 1911 Harry Mackalone was hired to run a Parisian bar called Clancy's. The eponymous Clancy had fled New York following a thwarted horse-racing scam, bringing his bar, piece by piece, from Manhattan's East Side to Paris. After the Great War, Harry took over the bar and renamed it, hiring the legendary 'Pete' Petoit, inventor of the Bloody Mary. Harry's became the place to be for American expatriates and hip Europeans alike, and was immortalized in the writings of Ernest Hemingway and F. Scott Fitzgerald.

The Original Bloody Mary

2 measures vodka
dash of lemon juice
Worcestershire sauce, to taste
tomato juice, to top up
½ teaspoon cayenne pepper
salt and black pepper

Pour the vodka and lemon juice over ice in a highball glass, add a little Worcestershire sauce and top up with tomato juice. Season with salt and both peppers, stir to chill and garnish with lime wedges.

Enjoy a diverse selection
of Martini-style and
Champagne-charged cocktails

FRANCE

Le Loft *Cannes*

There is more to Cannes than just the annual film festival – seek out Le Loft on rue de Docteur Monod, right in the heart of La Croisette, the town centre. An ultra-contemporary lounge bar in the New York style, it boasts what are arguably the most comfortable sofas in Europe. The relaxed ambience and low-key music provide the perfect back-drop to a chic gathering of fun-loving folk enjoying a diverse selection of predominantly Martini-style cocktails and Champagne-charged concoctions.

Riviera Fizz

1½ measures sloe gin
½ measure lemon juice
½ measure sugar syrup
Champagne, to top up

Shake the sloe gin, lemon juice and syrup together in a cocktail shaker with ice and strain into a chilled Champagne flute. Top up with Champagne, stir and decorate with a lemon twist.

Zebra Square *Monte Carlo*

The best time to visit Zebra Square is during Grand Prix weekend. If you can get past the closely guarded door, you'll be witness to some of the most extravagant partying anywhere on the planet as visiting celebrities rub shoulders with the local glitterati. The spacious verandah, appointed with luxurious outdoor furniture, is the ideal vantage-point to conduct a bit of celebrity-spotting while you sample one of Zebra Square's tempting cocktails. Otherwise, it is a perfect place to enjoy the panoramic sea view and watch the yachts coming and going from the famous harbour.

Strawberry and Mint Daiquiri

3 strawberries

dash of strawberry syrup

6 mint leaves

2 measures golden rum

2 measures lime juice

Muddle the strawberries, syrup and mint leaves in the bottom of a cocktail shaker. Add the rum and lime juice, shake with ice and double strain into a chilled slim Martini glass. Garnish with a strawberry slice and an extra mint leaf.

SPAIN

Boadas *Barcelona*

This classic Catalan cocktail bar is just off Barcelona's busiest street, Las Ramblas. Founder Miguel Boadas learned his trade at Ernest Hemingway's favourite drinking joint, La Floridita in Havana, and the principles he laid down in the early 1950s are still apparent today. There is no cocktail list, just three or four tuxedoed bartenders expertly mixing anything you request. If in doubt, just order the special of the day and you won't be disappointed.

The Boadas Cocktail

1 measure white rum
1 measure red Dubonnet
1 measure orange Curaçao

Stir and strain into a small Martini glass and decorate with a cherry or two.

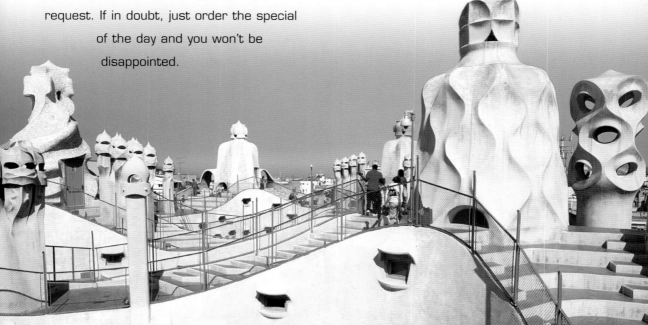

Chicote *Madrid*

Chicote stands out as an exquisite tribute to Madrid's drinking past. Opened in 1931 by Perico Chicote in order to 'mix drinks, lives and opinions', its décor has remained constant for over half a century. A favourite haunt of the city's bullfighters, this slice of history has also hosted many familiar names such as Frank Sinatra, Oliver Reed and Salvador Dali. The bartender insists that they make the best Mojitos in Spain. Their secret? 'Plenty of mint and modesty.' This was Hemingway's 'secret' recipe, divulged to the founder 60 years ago.

Pineapple Mojito

6 mint leaves

4 pineapple chunks

2 teaspoons brown sugar

2 measures golden rum

dash of pineapple juice

Muddle the mint, pineapple chunks and sugar in the bottom of a cocktail shaker. Add the rum and shake with ice. Strain into a glass filled with crushed ice, top up with the pineapple juice and stir. Garnish with a pineapple wedge and a mint sprig.

SPAIN

Bora Bora *Ibiza*

Bora Bora was born out of impromptu gatherings on the beach at Playa d'en Bossa in 1996, and was quickly followed by the legendary nightclub Space right next door. Bora Bora is a classic beach joint with hundreds of loungers for hire, live DJs every day of the week and a terraced dance floor where anything goes. It offers a long list of cocktails made from fresh natural juices. Known as the spot where the island's celebrities come to let their hair down, this bar has seen plenty of memorable parties in its time.

Bora Bora Sangria

½ measure Spanish brandy
4 measures Spanish red wine
dash of orange Curaçao
orange, apple and lemon wedges
cinnamon stick
4 measures lemonade, to top up

Combine the brandy, wine, orange Curaçao, fruit and cinnamon stick in a large jug. When ready to serve, top up the jug with the lemonade and stir. Pour into glasses with ice and garnish with slices of orange, lemon and apple.

Crystal Bar *Rome*

For many years, Rome's via Margutta was renowned for its bohemian enclave of artists and film-makers. These days, it is famous with hip Roman socialites and savvy expatriates for the Hotel Art and its Crystal Bar. Housed inside a former 19th-century chapel, the Hotel Art glories in vaulted ceilings, elaborate frescoes and stained glass windows. Across the cavernous lobby is a space-age pod that houses the Crystal Bar, with colour-coded, individually commissioned artwork adorning its walls. On Friday or Saturday night when it is in full swing, the bar serves up a delicious selection of cocktails until the small hours.

Grappa Manhattan

2 measures grappa

1 measure Martini Rosso

½ measure Maraschino liqueur

2 dashes of Angostura bitters

Stir together all the ingredients with ice in a mixing glass. Strain into a chilled Martini glass and decorate with an olive.

Harry's is a piece of drinking
history and has remained virtually
unchanged for decades

Harry's Bar *Venice*

Founded by the Cipriani family in 1931, Harry's is a piece of drinking history and has remained virtually unchanged for decades. The bar's list of habitués is endless, from Charlie Chaplin to Nicole Kidman. It even gets a mention in Ernest Hemingway's novel *Across the River and Into the Trees*. The interior is stylish and charming, as are the staff. Of course, the mention of Harry's invokes the Bellini, a delectable concoction that never tastes quite the same outside of its birthplace.

Bellini

1 measure white peach purée
Prosecco (Italian sparkling wine), to top up

Pour the peach purée and Prosecco into a flute, stir and decorate with a peach wedge.

GREECE

Cosmos *Athens*

Located beneath the Deste Foundation Centre for Contemporary Art, Cosmos strikes a near-perfect balance between cosy ambience and carefree luxury. However, do reserve a table ahead of your visit, as the chic bar area is permanently teeming with vibrant socialites eager to make themselves heard. Although the inevitable Ouzo is bound to appear in front of you at some point, Cosmos specializes in mixing classic cocktails with their own personal twist: the 'Pink' Mojito, the 'Lux' Daiquiri and the Bloody 'Maria' are a few of the classics given an Athenian spin.

Pink Mojito

6 mint leaves
½ lime
2 teaspoons sugar syrup
3 raspberries
1½ measures white rum
½ measure Chambord
cranberry juice, to top up

Muddle the mint, lime, syrup and raspberries in a highball glass. Add crushed ice and pour in the rum and Chambord. Stir well and top up with cranberry juice. Garnish with mint.

TURKEY

Laila *Istanbul*

Set on the banks of the Bosphorus, Laila has a bar and a club level, as well as the cushioned and candlelit open-air section by the water. The city's mosques provide a dramatic backdrop for the bar, making Laila a simply stunning drinking experience. The bartenders have created a varied selection of original Martinis, using fresh berries and a range of infused vodkas. The signature Laila Cocktail fuses the sweetness of mango and berries with a balancing citrus note.

Laila Cocktail

2 lime wedges

2 strawberries

4 blueberries

dash of mango purée

2 measures raspberry vodka

Muddle the lime wedges, berries and mango purée in the bottom of a cocktail shaker. Add the vodka with some ice cubes and shake vigorously. Double strain into a chilled Martini glass and garnish with 3 extra blueberries on a cocktail stick.

48

Dos Piranhas *Berlin*

Berlin has two distinct bar scenes. The quieter drinking dens of the eastern sector provide a contrast to the dazzle of the west. Dos Piranhas is in the heart of the west side, but the feel of the place is of comfortable intimacy. An enormous aquarium houses dozens of live piranhas. Feeding time is undeniably entertaining, but the enormous cocktail list is the real inspiration here. The bar offers over 200 exquisite recipes, with aged rum featuring heavily.

Berlin Blonde

1 measure dark rum

1 measure Cointreau

1 measure double cream

Pour the ingredients into a cocktail shaker. Shake with ice and double strain into a chilled Martini glass. Decorate with a sprinkle of ground cinnamon and a Maraschino cherry.

Bugsy's *Prague*

Bugsy's has almost mythical status in drinking circles of Eastern Europe, having set the standard by which classic cocktails in the region are judged. The voluminous drinks menu is 60 pages long, with 40 pages devoted to cocktails alone. The staff will talk you through it in English, and recommend cocktails to suit your taste. Bugsy's signature cocktail, the Almond Cigar, was invented by one of the bar's owners, Vaclav Vojir, and came second in Havana Rum's worldwide cocktail contest.

Almond Cigar

2 measures Havana 3-year-old rum

1 measure lime cordial

1 measure Amaretto

Pour the ingredients into a chilled cocktail shaker. Shake and strain into a chilled Martini glass. Garnish with a cinnamon stick and a twist of lime.

Most *Moscow*

A stone's throw from Red Square are the sidewalk terraces of Kuznetsky Most, Moscow's most fashionable district since the 18th century. The Most bar can be found on top of a modern building that looks as if it may well have arrived from outer space. The futuristic concept bar consists of sleek black leather and contrasting neon. Order from the fine list of Champagnes and cocktails, keeping in mind that Russia is not all about vodka and caviar.

Naked Vodkatini

3 measures frozen Stolichnaya vodka
½ measure Noilly Prat

Stir the ingredients together in a mixing glass and strain into a chilled Martini glass. Garnish with olives.

Combine the **sweetness**
of passion fruit with a
tangy citrus note...

Odeon *Oslo*

This classically styled bar is situated in the Majorstuen district and, once through the doors, you will find a lively, minimalist lounge packed with media types. The bartenders mix great cocktails using plenty of premium vodka, a favourite tipple in these northern regions. The signature cocktail, the Jenna J, is a long, refreshing drink with the sweetness of passion fruit balanced by fresh lemon and an underlying citrus note from the infused white rum.

Jenna J

2 measures Bacardi Limon

½ measure lemon juice

4 measures passion fruit juice

2 lime wedges

Build the ingredients over ice cubes in a highball glass. Squeeze the 2 lime wedges over the drink and then drop them in. Serve with long straws.

Café Opera *Stockholm*

Stockholm's hippest nightspot, located around the back of the Royal Opera House, offers a perfect bar ambience and splendid cocktails once you negotiate your way past the notoriously difficult door staff. Founded in 1980, Café Opera has retained many of the original 19th-century fittings, including an impressive painted ceiling by the artist Vicke Andrein, and boasts the longest bar in Stockholm. The cocktails are delicious, but can be a little pricey.

Kurant Blush

1½ measures Absolut Kurant vodka

½ measure Crème de Fraise

1 measure cranberry juice

2 lime wedges

Place all the ingredients in a cocktail shaker with some ice cubes and shake well. Double strain into a chilled Martini glass and decorate with a redcurrant on a cocktail stick.

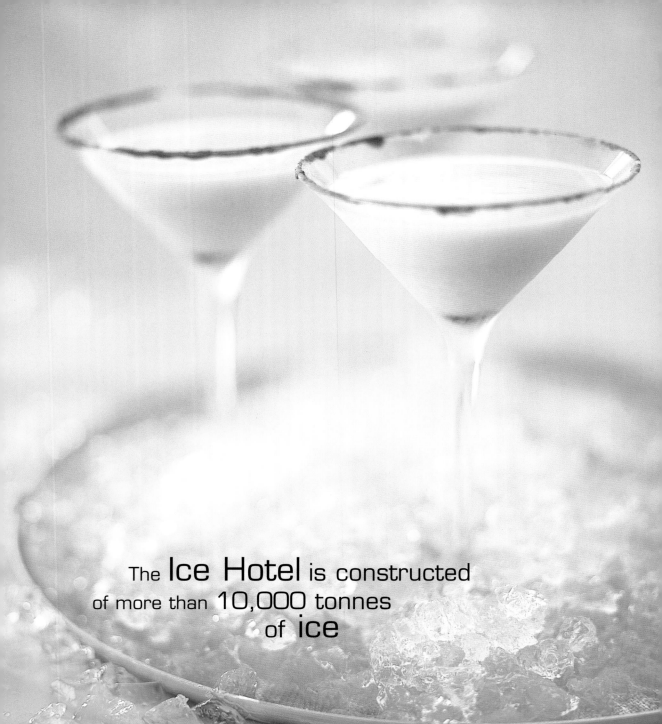

The **Ice Hotel** is constructed of more than **10,000 tonnes** of **ice**

Absolut Ice Bar *Jukkasjarvi*

Every autumn, the Lapland climate allows for the rebuilding of the Ice Hotel in Jukkasjarvi, constructed from more than 10,000 tonnes of ice. Even though the hotel averages an indoor temperature of -3°C (26°F), the exclusive Absolut Ice Bar is rated near the top of polls listing the world's favourite drinking establishments. The bar is redesigned every year, and the offerings on the cocktail list are also revamped annually. Don't bother asking for anything 'on the rocks' as each cocktail is served chilled to perfection in specially carved iceware.

Absolut Wonder

3 measures Absolut Vanilia vodka

1 measure Mozart white chocolate liqueur

Pour the vodka and liqueur into a chilled cocktail shaker. Shake and double strain into a chilled Martini glass, the rim of which has been dipped in lemon juice then grated chocolate. Finally, drop a cherry into the bottom of the glass to decorate.

AFRICA

Eclipse *Cape Town*

Part of a small international chain of bars, Eclipse overlooks the lush beaches of Camps Bay. Guests can enjoy a panorama of sand and sea from the bar while sipping cocktails that are imaginative, delicious and inexpensive. The quirky décor maximizes the feeling of space – low ottoman-style seating, white wood floors and huge windows – and the resident DJ plays ambient tunes to maintain the mood. Or you can venture out onto the terrace and enjoy the sounds of crashing waves as the Atlantic meets the Indian Ocean.

Eclipse

2 measures Jack Daniels whiskey

½ measure Chambord

½ measure lime juice

dash of sugar syrup

1 measure cranberry juice

1 measure raspberry purée

Place all the ingredients in a cocktail shaker with ice cubes. Shake and strain over crushed ice in a large highball glass. Serve with long straws and decorate with a raspberry and a lime wedge.

Baraza *Cape Town*

Taking its name from the Swahili word for 'meeting place', Baraza is one of South Africa's originals. The décor is inspired by the earthy colours, textures and culture of Zanzibar and, in particular, the Arab-influenced coastal trading post of Stone Town. This theme extends to the choice of music, the staff uniforms and the menus. With a tasty selection of cocktails and a delicious seafood menu, Baraza has become an institution in Cape Town. With DJs in residence on alternate evenings, Baraza provides the ideal venue for either a laid-back get-together or a full-on party.

Diamond Ring

dash of boiling water

1 teaspoon runny honey

3 basil leaves

1½ measures Zubrowka Bison
  Grass vodka

1 measure pressed apple juice

Stir the water, honey and basil leaves together in a cocktail shaker until well blended. Add the vodka, apple juice and some ice cubes. Shake well and double strain into a chilled Martini glass. Decorate with slices of apple.

Moyo *Johannesburg*

'My original idea was to do something authentic, to reflect contemporary African art, food and culture,' explains Jason Lurie, the mastermind behind Moyo. This masterpiece of African fusion has five levels looking down to the main stage, where an eclectic mix of African, jazz and drum displays entertain the crowds. Other musicians weave amongst the tables, serenading guests, and the waitresses and bar staff are dressed in full African regalia. Taking names from a number of native African languages, Moyo's cocktail list is relatively small, but invariably well made and original, served in jazzy local glassware.

Mbolero

2 lime wedges

2 measures gin

6 mint leaves

6 drops of orange bitters

dash of sugar syrup

Squeeze the lime wedges into a cocktail shaker, add the remaining ingredients and some ice cubes. Shake well and double strain into a chilled Martini glass. Decorate with a mint sprig.

Coconut Willy's *Mombasa*

Coconut Willy's is a palm-thatched bar that is part of the Serena Beach Hotel complex situated on Shanzu Beach. The entire complex is designed to resemble a 13th-century Swahili town, complete with marketplace and winding alleys. There is a wonderful swim-up bar where guests can order and enjoy their cocktails without ever having to leave the water. The cocktail of choice is the Strawberry Dawa, mixed in huge quantities in an enormous blender with heaps of crushed ice; it is the perfect antidote to the intense heat of the East African sun.

Strawberry Dawa

3 strawberries

1 lime, sliced

dash of strawberry syrup

2 measures lemon vodka

Muddle the strawberries, slices of lime and syrup in the base of a rocks glass, fill with crushed ice, add the vodka and stir to mix. Serve with the muddling stick if you have one and decorate with a split strawberry.

TANZANIA

Mangapwani Beach Club *Zanzibar*

Located on the northwest coast of Zanzibar, this beach paradise has a chequered past. Nearby are the so-called Slave Caves, where slaves were hidden after laws changed abolishing slavery. Mangapwani Beach Club overlooks the teeming waters of the Indian Ocean and guests enjoy an exotic selection of well-known tropical cocktails at tables shaded by a thatched awning. A menu of fresh seafood from Zanzibar's waters is also offered.

Piña Colada

2 measures rum

2 teaspoons lime juice

2 measures coconut cream

1 scoop vanilla ice cream

2 measures pineapple juice

Place all the ingredients in a blender with some ice and process on high speed until well mixed. Serve in a large hurricane glass with long straws and a wedge of fresh pineapple to decorate.

KENYA

The Carnivore *Nairobi*

Open-air and set amongst landscaped gardens, The Carnivore is a *nyama choma* (barbecued meat) restaurant and is one of few places licensed to serve gazelle, giraffe or zebra as a dish. Both The Carnivore bar and nightclub are extremely popular and it was here that the famous Dawa cocktail was first created. In Swahili the word 'Dawa' means a drink somewhere between a medicine and a magic potion. Traditionally the drink is served with a small green wooden masher so that you can release more lime juice and thus adjust the flavour of your Dawa to your liking.

Dawa

1 lime, quartered and thickly sliced

1 tablespoon thick honey

1 teaspoon caster sugar

2 measures vodka

Place the lime slices, honey and sugar in a heavy-based rocks glass and crush lightly together with a spoon. Add some ice and pour over the vodka.

NIGERIA

Calabash Bar *Lagos*

To call Lagos bustling is an understatement. As the commercial hub of Nigeria, it is a teeming city whose roads seem to be in a constant state of gridlock. This makes the rooftop Calabash Bar, on top of Le Meridien Eko Hotel, the ideal retreat for a refreshing cocktail and a dip in the adjoining swimming pool. The bar provides stunning views across the city and, with a bit of luck, they'll be playing the music of such famed Lagos musicians as Fela Kuti, Sunny Ade or Sonny Okosun. Notable on the cocktail list are the rum punch and the deliciously refreshing and original white wine sangria.

'White' Sangria

2 large glasses of dry white wine
2 measures lemon vodka
2 measures peach schnapps
2 measures peach purée
slices of apple, lime, lemon and peach
1 measure lemon juice
1 measure lime juice
lemonade, to top up

12 hours before serving, place the wine, vodka, Schnapps and peach purée in a jug with the fruit slices and chill. Just before serving, add some ice cubes, the fruit juices and top up with lemonade. Serve from the jug into rocks glasses.

The Calabash Bar is
the **ideal** retreat for a
refreshing cocktail and a dip in the
adjoining swimming pool

MAURITIUS

The Golf Club Bar

Named after a French vessel that was shipwrecked here in 1744, Le Saint Geran resort is on a private estate on the Belle Mare peninsula of Mauritius. The Golf Club Bar has a panoramic view of the spectacular nine-hole links course designed by Gary Player and also has its own signature cocktail, the Green Island Fragrance. If visiting the island, it is easy to appreciate the aptness of this cocktail.

Green Island Fragrance

1½ measures vodka

½ measure Midori

1 measure lemon juice

1 measure pineapple juice

dash of sugar syrup

1 lemon wedge

Pour the ingredients into a cocktail shaker with some ice cubes. Shake and strain over ice in a highball glass. Squeeze the lemon wedge over the drink, drop it in and serve with straws.

EGYPT

La Bodega *Cairo*

La Bodega is a challenge to find: look out for a small sign above the door bearing the word Baehler (after the manager Charles Baehler), then head upstairs to the bar and restaurant. Designed in the style of the Roaring Twenties, La Bodega is full of commissioned pieces by local and foreign artists. A romantic view of the Nile and great cocktail classics produced by smartly attired bartenders make for a completely delightful experience. Particularly noteworthy cocktails are the Natural Daiquiri and an Old-fashioned made with a small measure of the local rum.

Rum Old-Fashioned

dash of Angostura bitters
dash of lime bitters
1 teaspoon caster sugar
½ measure water
2 measures white rum
½ measure dark rum

Stir the bitters, sugar and water in the bottom of a heavy-based rocks glass with 1 ice cube until the sugar dissolves. Add the white rum, stir and add 2 more ice cubes. Add the dark rum, and stir once again. Decorate with a lime twist.

ASIA

Indigo *Mumbai*

The restaurant at Indigo was recently voted one of the top 100 in the world; however, the distinctive décor and the delicious (and very potent) cocktails are the real highlight at this Mumbai nightspot. On the floor above the starkly minimalist restaurant is Indigo's terrace and cigar bar, the latter decorated in the deepest blue – hence the name. Indigo reflects the colourful, vibrant culture of the city and you're likely to spot a few top Bollywood stars either perched at the bar or gyrating wildly on the dance floor.

Strawberry and Hazelnut Lassi

3 strawberries

⅓ banana

1 measure Frangelico

1 measure Baileys

2 measures yogurt

3 mint leaves

Place all the ingredients in a blender and process with a small scoop of crushed ice until smooth. Serve in a tall sling glass and decorate with a mint sprig.

Fresh ingredients for
the cocktails are selected
from the markets each day

Solypse Café *Goa*

The Solypse Café is the ideal pit-stop for a late afternoon drink before heading up to the Nine Bar on the cliff-top above Ozran Beach to check out the sunset. They serve a wonderful range of fresh fruit cocktails – mostly rum- and vodka-based, although non-alcoholic varieties are also available. The fresh ingredients are selected from the markets each day, so the menu changes according to what is in season. Made frappé-style with crushed ice in a blender, these concoctions are a reviving antidote to the intense humidity of Goa.

Frozen Mango Daiquiri

½ mango, peeled and stoned

1 measure lime juice

1 teaspoon powdered white sugar

2 measures white rum

Place all the ingredients in a blender and process with a small scoop of crushed ice until smooth. Serve in any large glass (they are not fussy at Solypse), and decorate with slices of ripe mango.

MALDIVES

Naiboli Bar at the Banyan Tree *Vabbinfaru*

Cast away on a secluded coral atoll in the Maldives archipelago, Vabbinfaru Island is the epitome of tropical paradise, particularly at sunset. It provides the perfect backdrop for the Naiboli Bar, which serves a small but well-chosen selection of crisp white wines, Champagnes, Asian beers and some delicious cocktails. The Mojitos are worthy of particular mention: made with care, plenty of ice and a variety of fresh fruit flavours, the choice depends on who is running the bar on any particular day. The star of the bar, however, is the Sea Breeze made with freshly squeezed pink grapefruit juice.

Sea Breeze

2 measures vodka

4 measures cranberry juice

2 measures pink grapefruit juice

2 lime wedges

Pour the vodka and fruit juices into a large glass over ice. Squeeze over the lime wedges and stir lightly before serving.

'Shanghai is **ready**
for a bar for **grown-ups**'

CHINA

The Glamour Bar *Shanghai*

'Shanghai is ready for a bar for grown-ups,' announced owner Michelle Garnaut just prior to the 2001 opening of her Glamour Bar as part of world-famous M-on-the-Bund restaurant. And glamorous it certainly is. Reminiscent of a 1930s Hollywood film set, the shimmering interior features silver-dipped columns, curtains of sparkling crystal and fine detailing in copper, nickel and bronze. An extensive, leather-bound list of classic and contemporary cocktails sits on top of the gleaming metal bar; if you are in any doubt, simply order the signature Glamour Martini.

The Glamour Martini

1½ measures vodka

½ measure cherry brandy

2 measures blood orange juice

½ measure lime juice

Pour all the ingredients into a cocktail shaker with some ice cubes, shake well and strain into a chilled Martini glass. Decorate with a twist of orange.

Aria Bar *Beijing*

Aria is in the downstairs lobby of the China World Hotel. A sumptuous mahogany spiral staircase leads into this den of relaxed and dimly lit elegance. There are two sections to the cocktail list – Classics and Bubbles – and the bartenders are continually finding new ways of flavouring Champagne, using home-made fruit syrups and infused spirits. Aria's signature cocktail is a simple twist on the Champagne Classic, a rich herbal taste, finishing with a lasting orange note.

Aria Classic

1 brown sugar cube
3 drops of Angostura bitters
1 measure Grand Marnier
Champagne, to top up

Place the sugar cube in the bottom of a chilled flute glass and soak in the Angostura bitters. Add the Grand Marnier and stir briefly. Top up with Champagne and decorate with an orange twist.

JAPAN

Montoak *Tokyo*

Montoak is situated on a discreet side street off the bustling Omotesando Avenue. There are no signs outside the bar marking its presence so look out for the three-storey smoked-glass building with a terrace on the second floor. The minimalist menu offers a selection of deluxe coffees, flavoured sakes and sumptuous cocktails, both classic and contemporary; try the cooling but deceptively powerful Cucumber Saketini.

Cucumber Saketini

2½ measures cucumber-infused sake
1½ measures gin
½ measure orange Curaçao

Stir all the ingredients together in a mixing glass with some ice cubes until thoroughly chilled. Strain into a chilled Martini glass and decorate with peeled cucumber slices.

CHINA

Dragon-i *Hong Kong*

Decorated with phoenix-print lanterns and cream leather furnishings, the Dragon-i is designed to reflect a fusion of ancient Chinese and Japanese influences. Split into a dining area (the Red Room) and a public bar with dance floor (the Playground), Dragon-i is a popular night spot for both drinkers and diners. The cocktails, along with the sake, are known to be strong; the Dragon's Fire is fresh and fiery. Dragon-i is also a good place for celebrity-spotting – local superstar Jackie Chan has been known to pop in from time to time.

Dragon's Fire

1½ measures Absolut Mandarin vodka

1 measure Cointreau

dash of lime juice

1 measure cranberry juice

Pour all the ingredients into a cocktail shaker with some ice cubes. Shake and double strain into a chilled Martini glass. Decorate with an orange twist.

Space-age furniture adorns the club and **beds** are **suspended** from the walls

Bed Supper Club *Bangkok*

The Bed Supper Club extends an open invitation to 'wine, dine and recline' in what looks like a vast intergalactic spaceship. The blindingly white décor and candy-coloured lighting casts an otherworldly glow. Beds are suspended from the walls and space-age furniture adds to the theme. The staff are dressed to fit the scene, while the cocktails are named and presented with this sci-fi theme in mind, using clean, unfussy garnishes and striking glassware.

Horizon

1½ measures Zubrowka Bison
  Grass vodka
½ measure Xante pear liqueur
1 measure pressed apple juice
1 teaspoon passion fruit liqueur
dash of lemon juice

Pour all the ingredients into a cocktail shaker with some ice cubes. Shake and double strain into a chilled Martini glass. Decorate with a lemon twist.

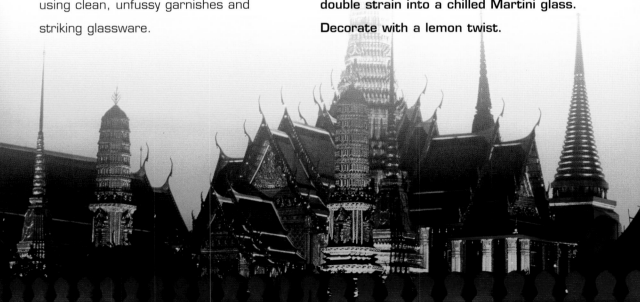

Rasta Baby *Koh Samui*

Set on Bophut Beach, the Rasta Baby has a perfect location, secluded yet easy to find and close enough to the sea to grab a cooling dip at any time. The bar is as easy-going as its name suggests and is part of a small resort complex offering basic accommodation in the form of beach huts. A selection of cocktails by the pitcher is on offer from the bar, along with ice-cold local beers and traditional Thai dishes. The resident DJ provides the vibes, the bartenders put on a show of fire juggling, and the party usually goes on until dawn.

Rollin' Stoned

2 measures Thai whisky

dash of banana liqueur

dash of raspberry liqueur

dash of lime juice

2 measures orange juice

2 measures pineapple juice

Pour all the ingredients into a cocktail shaker with some ice cubes. Shake and strain into an ice-filled highball glass. Garnish with slices of orange and cherries and serve with long straws.

For the price of your 'Sing Sling',
you get to keep the glass

SINGAPORE

The Long Bar *Singapore City*

Home to one of the most famous cocktails ever invented, The Long Bar at Raffles Hotel will forever occupy a key position in the history of cocktails. The house speciality, the Singapore Sling, was first concocted by bartender Mr Ngiam Tong Boon in 1910. Since then, The Long Bar has become a tourist magnet – so much so that, for the price of your 'Sing Sling', you get to keep the glass. Another grand tradition here is to discard your peanut shells on the floor – a true sign of hospitality and a rare treat given the notoriously stringent littering laws of Singapore.

Singapore Sling

1 measure gin
½ measure cherry brandy
¼ measure Cointreau
¼ measure Dom Benedictine
½ measure grenadine
½ measure lime juice
5 measures pineapple juice
dash of Angostura bitters

Pour all the ingredients into a cocktail shaker with some ice. Shake and strain over ice cubes in a sling glass. Decorate with a slice of pineapple and a cherry.

Mafia Bar *Seoul*

The fact that this upmarket bar is so difficult to track down has helped the Mafia Bar gain an air of exclusivity. This is reinforced by its distinctive black interior lined with dark velvet and low lighting. A notable lack of fresh fruit or fruit purées in the bar is intentional; instead, a list of classic pure spirit concoctions fits the mood perfectly. The simple Mafia Martini is rum-based with a delicious sweetness and a citrus twist.

Mafia Martini

2 measures golden rum
½ measure Chambord
1 measure apple juice

Pour the ingredients into a cocktail shaker with some ice cubes. Shake briefly and double strain into a chilled Martini glass. Decorate with a lime twist.

The walk up to the Jati Bar
leads you through towering
vegetation and the surreal
sounds of the jungle

Jati Bar *Bali*

The Jati Bar is part of the Four Seasons Resort in the central highlands of Bali. The décor is comfortably minimalist with ceiling-high palms, wicker furniture and enormous fans. The bar has a small but choice selection of infused vodkas, using simple Asian flavours such as lemon grass, lime and ginger. Like its deliciously simple cocktails, the walk up to the Jati is also impressive; through towering vegetation and the surreal sounds of the jungle, this luxurious bar is the perfect balance between wilderness and modern opulence.

Lime Fizz

1 lime wedge
1 measure lime vodka
1 measure orange juice
Champagne, to top up

Squeeze the lime wedge into a cocktail shaker and add the vodka and orange juice with some ice cubes. Shake very briefly and double strain into a chilled Champagne flute. Top up with Champagne and decorate with lime twists.

AUSTRALASIA

Hemmesphere *Sydney*

'Cocktails have taken off in Sydney in the past year, it's a real cult,' said Justin Hemmes, owner of Hemmesphere in 2002. Hemmesphere opened its doors days before the Sydney 2000 Olympics and, since then, has gone from strength to strength. Using a combination of wonderfully fresh produce, their skills and imagination, the bar team mix some of the finest cocktails in Australia. Hemmesphere is the slightly more hip younger brother of the Establishment bar downstairs and, while it is officially a private members' club, everyone is welcome to join.

Watermelon Martini

1 lime wedge
4 chunks of watermelon
1½ measures vodka
½ measure Passoa (passion-fruit liqueur)
dash of cranberry juice

Squeeze the lime wedge into a cocktail shaker, add some ice cubes and the remaining ingredients and shake vigorously. Double strain into a chilled Martini glass and decorate with a wedge of watermelon.

AUSTRALIA

Mink *Melbourne*

Mink has been accurately described as a 'vodka and velvet bar'. There are 43 vodka varieties on the menu along with a small but excellent cocktail selection to be sipped appreciatively on plush velvet seating in small curtained alcoves, surrounded by decadent murals. Located in the basement beneath the Prince of Wales Hotel, it is a haven for late-night antics without the pretentious attitudes often associated with this type of venue. The DJs play an eclectic mix of fresh and funky tunes most nights of the week.

Slinky Mink

½ measure raspberry purée

dash of sugar syrup

2 teaspoons lime juice

Champagne, to top up

Build the purée, syrup and lime juice in the bottom of a chilled flute glass. Add Champagne to top up, stir lightly and decorate with a lime twist.

Geisha Bar *Perth*

In the past, Perth was better known for its wine than for its cocktails due to the southwest's perfect vineyard conditions. However, in recent years more and more cocktail bars and clubs have been set up by professional bartenders from overseas, resulting in the rapid expansion of one of the world's remotest cities. Geisha Bar can be found in Northbridge and is a charming, cosy little den with alluring Japanese décor and an interesting menu of well-mixed cocktails. The atmosphere is warm and friendly with a host of local and international DJs providing a good range of music.

Lemon grass Collins

2 measures lemon grass vodka
½ measure vanilla liqueur
dash of lemon juice
dash of sugar syrup
ginger beer, to top up

Fill a large Collins glass with crushed ice. Then add, in this order, the vodka, liqueur, lemon juice and syrup. Stir, add more ice and top up with ginger beer. Decorate with lemon slices and serve with long straws.

Coast *Auckland*

Despite its panoramic views out over Auckland Harbour, it is still hard to believe that the Coast bar and lounge occupy what used to be the harbour master's offices. It has been transformed through slick minimalist design and cool modern furnishings. The bartenders are very adaptable and will cater for all tastes, using their vast knowledge of cocktails. There are three distinct bars on the premises – the Main Bar, the Black Bar for dancing and the Pink Bar for chilling out.

Gin Garden

¼ **of cucumber, peeled and chopped**
½ **measure elderflower cordial**
2 **measures gin**
1 **measure pressed apple juice**

Muddle the cucumber in the bottom of a cocktail shaker with the elderflower cordial. Add the gin, apple juice and some ice cubes. Shake and double strain into a chilled Martini glass and decorate with peeled cucumber slices.

Bardeaux *Queenstown*

From late June to September, the winter months, travellers from around the world arrive in Queenstown to enjoy the nearby ski slopes. The Bardeaux is a dimly lit lounge with deep leather lounge suites and huge suede bean bags, all warmed by an enormous open fireplace. Reputed to make the best cocktails in New Zealand, Bardeaux's bar team have put together an extensive cocktail list with a heavy bias towards vodka- and bourbon-based creations.

Swallow Dive

1 measure honey vodka

1 measure Chambord

1 measure lime juice

4 raspberries

Place all the ingredients in a cocktail shaker and add some ice cubes. Shake well and strain over crushed ice in a rocks glass. Top with more crushed ice and decorate with 2 extra raspberries.

Beachcomber Sand Bar *Mamanuca*

Beachcomber Island is a small coral atoll situated in the heart of the Mamanucas group of islands, a catamaran-ride away from the main Fijian island of Viti Levu. The island is so tiny that it comes as no surprise to discover that their bar is right on the beach – ideally situated for sunbathers and surfers. It is stocked with a mix of freshly squeezed juices, draught beers and suitably tropical cocktails, often garnished like a hanging garden. Don't underestimate the power of their Illusion, decked with melon, cherries and often the ubiquitous paper umbrella.

Illusion

2 measures vodka
½ measure Midori
½ measure Triple Sec
½ measure lime juice
lemonade, to top up

Pour the vodka, Midori, Triple Sec and lime juice into a cocktail shaker and add ice cubes. Shake and strain over ice in a large hurricane glass or a hollowed pineapple shell. Top up with lemonade, stir and decorate with melon slices, lemon slices and cherries arranged on a cocktail stick. Serve with long straws.

SOUTH
+ CENTRAL
AMERICA

BRAZIL

Baretto *São Paulo*

By far the most famous Brazilian cocktail is the Caiparinha, whose main ingredient is the local liquor cachaça. Apart from beer, cachaça is the most popular drink in Brazil, with over 4,000 brands available and more than 1 billion bottles sold each year. It is also used to make a less well-known cocktail called the Batida. There can be no finer place to sample a Caiparinha than in the elegant São Paulo retreat of Baretto. With its cream leather furnishings and subtle lighting, Baretto maintains a warmth and glamour night and day.

Caiparinha

1 lime, quartered

2 teaspoons cane sugar

2 measures cachaça

Muddle the lime quarters and sugar together in the base of a rocks glass. Fill it with crushed ice and pour over the cachaça. Stir and add more ice as desired.

Garota de Ipanema *Rio de Janeiro*

Rio de Janeiro has one of the most dramatic settings of any world city, with Sugar Loaf Mountain as a backdrop and Copacabana and Ipanema beaches providing the stage. Named after the classic song written by two of its regulars, Garota de Ipanema ('Girl from Ipanema') is a popular beach front bar that serves a range of exotic cocktails. The tropical attire worn by the staff suits the cocktails they produce – concoctions based on Brazil's national drinks, the Caiparinha and the Batida. The less-famous Batida may soon enjoy a surge in popularity thanks to delicious varieties using fruits such as guava, pineapple, strawberry and passion fruit.

Batida Maracuja

2 measures cachaça

2 passion fruit

1 measure sugar syrup

1 measure lemon juice

Place the cachaça, passion fruit pulp, syrup and lemon juice into a cocktail shaker and add some ice cubes. Shake and strain into a highball glass filled with crushed ice. Decorate with slices of lemon and serve with long straws.

Maury Bar *Lima*

The claim to fame of this neo-classical lounge bar is that it invented the legendary Pisco Sour. First created in the early 1900s, this cocktail is now mixed all over the world. As with many classic cocktails, the invention came about because Pisco (a grape brandy) was often of a raw, low quality. It was rendered more drinkable when mixed with other ingredients – in this case a simple sweet and sour mix with aromatic Angostura and an egg white to give it body and a silken finish.

Original Pisco Sour

2 measures Pisco

1 measure lemon juice

2 teaspoons caster sugar

1 egg white

3 drops of Angostura bitters

Place the Pisco, lemon juice, sugar and egg white in a cocktail shaker with some ice cubes. Shake and strain into an ice-filled rocks glass. Add the drops of bitters to the drink's frothy head.

Hotel Explora *San Pedro de Atacama*

There is nowhere better suited to testing the Chilean Pisco Sour's thirst-quenching properties than the Atacama Desert, a region of volcanoes, geysers and chalk cliffs. At the splendidly isolated Hotel Explora, cocktails are served every evening and guests are invited to sample the bar's unique twist on Chile's – and Peru's – national drink. The Pisco Sours produced in Chile and Peru are marked by a difference not only in ingredients, but also texture and taste. The most significant exclusion from the Chilean variety is the egg white, resulting in a fresh sorbet texture.

Atacama Pisco Sour

1½ measures Pisco

½ measure blended Scotch whisky

1 measure lemon juice

1 measure sugar syrup

Pour all the ingredients into a blender and process with a small scoop of crushed ice until smooth. Serve in a coupette glass, decorated with grated lemon rind.

Mundo Bizarro *Buenos Aires*

Buenos Aires is not a city for those who believe in early nights. The locals think nothing of sitting down to dinner at 10pm, then moving on to their favourite night-spot for drinking and dancing until the small hours. Mundo Bizarro is the bohemian epitome of cool in social circles of Buenos Aires, and serves the finest cocktails in town. Low lighting and wall-mounted candles illuminate this intimate hideaway. The contemporary Latin music takes a back seat to the hum of conversation in what sounds like a million different languages and accents.

Bossanova

2 measures white rum

½ measure Galliano

½ measure apricot brandy

4 measures pressed apple juice

1 measure lime juice

½ measure sugar syrup

Pour the ingredients into a cocktail shaker and add some ice cubes. Shake and strain into an ice-filled highball glass. Decorate with split lime wedges and serve with long straws.

The **lock-ins** at Monoloco

serve as a **proving ground**

for new, **inventive** concoctions

Monoloco *Antigua*

Every foreign traveller making their way through Central America seems to spend an afternoon sampling simple, classic cocktails and great Mexican-style food in this delightful bar at the end of a covered walkway. Although Monoloco is essentially a sports bar, the drinks are fantastic and the regular 'everyone-welcome' after-hours lock-ins serve as a proving ground for new, inventive concoctions. If the American owner is in the right mood, you can jump up onto the roof of the bar, from where you can enjoy awe-inspiring views of the three volcanoes ringing the city.

Monoloco Zombie

1 measure white rum

1 measure Navy rum

½ measure apricot brandy

½ measure orange Curaçao

2 measures orange juice

2 measures pineapple juice

½ measure lime juice

dash of grenadine

½ measure overproof rum

Pour all the ingredients, except the overproof rum, into a cocktail shaker and add some ice cubes. Shake and strain over ice in a large hurricane glass. Top with the remaining rum and decorate with wedges of pineapple.

La Capilla *Tequila*

La Capilla is in the historic town of Tequila, home of Mexico's national spirit. The oldest bar in town, it is owned and operated by Don Javier, who has been a bartender for 55 years. La Capilla is small with just a few bar stools and tables and, essentially, only one drink on the menu – the Batanga. Most of the regulars make their own and between them there exists an honours system of payment – Don Javier will ask how many they've had and charge accordingly. However, be warned – the Batanga can be very addictive!

Batanga

1 Mexican lime
rock salt
2 measures Tequileno Blanco tequila
Mexican cola, to top up

Cut the tip off the lime, make a slit in its side, dip in rock salt and run it round the edge of a sturdy rocks glass. Fill the glass with ice cubes and add the tequila. Squeeze out half the lime juice then, with the knife used to cut the lime, stir the drink while topping up with Mexican cola.

MEXICO

Cosmo *Mexico City*

Cosmo is a shining example of the recent wave of lounge bars to hit the Mexican capital. Martinis and flavoured Margaritas occupy most of the menu space, with skilled local bar staff making the drinks and American management overseeing the super-friendly surroundings of one of the city's hottest bars. Cosmo is also a magnet for the city's dance crowd, who flock to hear guest DJs from around the world.

Grand Margarita

1 lime wedge
rock salt
1½ measures silver tequila
1 measure Grand Marnier
1 measure lime juice

Moisten the rim of a coupette glass with the lime wedge and coat the outside edge with salt. Pour the tequila, Grand Marnier and lime juice into a cocktail shaker and shake with ice. Double strain into the glass and decorate with a lime wedge.

CARIBBEAN

140

Foxy's Tamarind Bar *Jost van Dyke*

The island of Jost van Dyke had no pavements until recently and all power is supplied by generators, giving visitors the feeling of having stepped back in time. An old-fashioned welcome is also offered by entertainer and local conservationist Philicianno 'Foxy' Callwood, owner of Foxy's Tamarind Bar. The New Year's Eve parties held at the bar are the stuff of legends, and the population of the island swells from around 200 to tens of thousands. For the Millennium celebrations, the number of guests ran to six figures, and it was for this spectacular occasion that Foxy's Millennium Punch was created.

Foxy's Millennium Punch

1½ measures white rum

1 measure dark rum

2 measures cranberry juice

2 measures guava juice

½ measure lime juice

Pour all the ingredients over ice in a large highball glass and stir. Decorate with slices of pineapple and lime.

Le Select *Gustavia*

Immortalized in the song 'Cheeseburger in Paradise' by the eccentric country singer Jimmy Buffett, Le Select is a popular hangout for tourists and locals alike. It is also the chosen summer retreat for many celebrities such as Brad Pitt and Jennifer Aniston, to name a few. The best type of stargazing, however, is done while staring into the night sky and sipping on one of Le Select's numerous varieties of Rum Punch. Each barman at Le Select has his own recipes, which has led to the fantastic variety available on the menu.

Parrot's Head Punch

1½ measures vodka

1 measure passion fruit liqueur

2 measures watermelon juice

1 measure cranberry juice

1½ measures pink grapefruit juice

Build all the ingredients over ice in a hurricane glass and decorate with slices of grapefruit. Serve with long straws.

After Dark *Christchurch*

St Lawrence Gap isn't a gap as such, but a long stretch of beach-front road where some of Christchurch's most popular restaurants, bars and clubs are found. The main bar at After Dark is reputedly the longest single piece of polished mahogany in the world, and folklore has it that there are no two bottles the same behind the bar. An army of bartenders and waitresses serve ice-cold beers and enormous jugs of tropical cocktails to thirsty crowds, while the dance floor moves to the Bajan rhythms of local bands.

After Dark Crush

2 measures Barbadian rum

½ measure Koko Kanu (coconut rum)

½ measure vanilla syrup

1 measure coconut cream

soda water, to top up

Fill a sling glass with crushed ice, then add, in order, the rums, syrup and coconut cream. Stir and top up with soda. Add more ice and decorate with cherries. Serve with long straws.

Rick's Café *Westmorland*

Virtually every tour leaving Negril Beach ends at Rick's, which is famous around the world for its cliff-jumping opportunities and glorious sunsets. The diving cliff might not be as intimidating as those at Acapulco, but it's probably best to take the plunge before you start sampling the house cocktails! Top of the menu is undoubtedly the Planter's Punch, which was created by Fred L. Myers in the late 19th century. Rick's has transformed this classic drink into something a little 'juicier' by substituting pineapple juice for water, so feel free to either stick with tradition or go the modern route.

Planter's Punch

2 measures Myer's Jamaican Planter's Punch rum

4 drops of Angostura bitters

½ measure lime juice

2 measures chilled water

1 measure sugar syrup

Pour all the ingredients into a cocktail shaker and add some ice cubes. Shake and strain into an ice-filled highball glass. Decorate with slices of orange and lime.

El Floridita *Havana*

As you enter El Floridita, you will notice a roped-off bar stool, left empty in memory of Ernest Hemingway. Although often heaving with tourists, this bar is still one of the best. Jesus Rodriguez Fernandez is the current head bartender and a student of Rolando Quinones, the manager who used to mix Hemingway his famed Papa Doble with no sugar and a triple helping of rum. A more user-friendly version would be to include half a measure of sugar syrup and two measures of rum.

The Papa Doble

3 measures white rum
½ measure maraschino liqueur
1 measure lime juice
1½ measures grapefruit juice

Pour all the ingredients into a blender with a scoop of crushed ice and blend until smooth. Serve in a highball glass with grapefruit wedges. This drink can be sweetened to taste with sugar syrup, although Hemingway never would.

'My Daiquiri at El Floridita
and my Mojito at
La Bodeguita del Medio'

CUBA

La Bodeguita del Medio *Havana*

'My Daiquiri at El Floridita and my Mojito at La Bodeguita del Medio' is a quote often attributed to Ernest Hemingway. In fact, it was coined by Fernando B. Campaomer, a local journalist and drinking partner of 'Papa'. Well into his eighties and still living in Havana, Campaomer joked that the Bodeguita's owner needed a Hemingway quote in order to become famous and 'something like that' should do. Although this bar is quite touristy, it's worth the visit if only for the Mojito.

Mojito

8 mint leaves

½ lime

2 teaspoons cane sugar

2½ measures white rum

soda water, to top up

Muddle the mint leaves, lime and sugar in the bottom of a highball glass and fill with crushed ice. Add the rum, stir and top up with soda water. Decorate with mint sprigs.

Basil's Bar *Mustique*

Over a quarter of a century on, Basil's has earned its place on the list of the world's greatest beach bars. It has been over 30 years since Basil Charles was first brought to Mustique by the owner of the island, Lord Glenconner, to work as a bartender in his famous Cotton House hotel. His bar is built on stilts over Macaroni Beach, and many of the exotic cocktails, such as the Mango Sling, are based on tropical fruit.

Basil's Mango Sling

1½ measures vodka

1½ measures mango purée

1 measure apricot liqueur

½ measure lemon juice

dash of sugar syrup

soda water, to top up

Pour the vodka, mango, apricot liqueur, lemon juice and syrup into a cocktail shaker and add some ice cubes. Shake very briefly and strain over crushed ice in a sling glass. Top up with soda and decorate with slices of ripe mango.

Over a quarter of a century on, Basil's
has earned its place
on the list of the world's
greatest beach bars

Miss Emily's Blue Bee Bar *Green Turtle Cay*

An unprepossessing, sky-blue building in Green Turtle Cay is the birthplace of the legendary Goombay Smash. The drink's inventor, the late Miss Emily Cooper (pictured below), never partook of the cocktail herself because of her Christian beliefs, but that didn't stop her from running one of the most popular drinking posts in the Bahamas. Miss Emily passed on her secret recipe for Goombay Smash to her daughter, so you'll have to travel to the Blue Bee to try the genuine article.

Goombay Smash

1½ measures coconut rum

1 measure cachaça

½ measure apricot brandy

½ measure lime juice

4 measures pineapple juice

Pour all the ingredients into a cocktail shaker and add some ice cubes. Shake and strain over ice in a large glass. Decorate with pineapple slices, a lime twist and cherries.

NORTH AMERICA

158

Elbo Room *Fort Lauderdale*

Drive along the beachfront at Fort Lauderdale and it is hard to miss this two-storey, flamingo-pink building. Established in 1938, the Elbo Room was popular with sailors during World War Two. By the 1960s it attracted college students on their annual Spring Break holiday. In the early 1990s it was awarded the city's first outdoor drinking licence. The cocktails are big, brash and often inexpensive, made with a large dose of bar theatrics and plenty of all-American attitude.

Bay Breeze

4 measures cranberry juice

2 measures vodka

2 measures pineapple juice

Fill a highball glass with ice cubes and pour in the cranberry juice. Shake the vodka with the pineapple juice in a chilled cocktail shaker and pour gently over the cranberry juice. Decorate with lime wedges and serve with long straws.

Nikki Beach Bar *Miami*

Nikki Beach Bar is at one of the most prestigious addresses in Miami: 1 Ocean Drive. It is a beach bar, restaurant and club all rolled into one fantastic venue and doused in the relentlessly perfect climate of South Beach. French designer Stephane Dupoux used the classic beach clubs of Europe as inspiration, but introduced a multi-cultural ethnic feel to the design. Unlike most bars in this part of the world, Nikki Beach has a thoughtful cocktail list, with a heavy rum influence and plenty of fresh tropical fruit.

Limon Mojito

1 lime, quartered
2 teaspoons brown sugar
8 mint leaves
2 measures Bacardi Limon
soda water, to top up (optional)

Muddle the lime quarters, sugar and mint in the bottom of a highball glass. Fill the glass with crushed ice and add the rum. Stir and top up with soda water if you like. Decorate with slices of lemon and lime and serve with long straws.

Sky Bar *Los Angeles*

Bars go in and out of fashion in Los Angeles, but the Sky Bar on the roof of the Mondrian Hotel always seems to have its celebrities. Designed by Randy Gerber, husband of supermodel Cindy Crawford, it is a mostly open-air venue with swimming pool, chaises longues, a roving cigarette girl and views over LA. The bar team has put together an extensive list, but the Apple Martini, the first cocktail ever made here, remains the most popular.

Apple Martini

2 measures vodka
1 measure apple Schnapps
1 tablespoon apple purée
dash of lime juice
pinch of ground cinnamon

Pour all the ingredients into a cocktail shaker and add some ice cubes. Shake and double strain into a chilled Martini glass. Decorate with red apple wedges.

The Apple Martini was the
first cocktail ever made
at the Sky Bar

Bemelmans Bar *New York*

A real taste of old New York, Bemelmans Bar at the Carlyle Hotel is a wonderful place to drop in and relax after a stroll around Central Park. The bar takes its name from the children's author and artist Ludwig Bemelmans, who also devised the animal mural that adorns the bar. The menu is inspiring and originally compiled by legendary mixologist and 'king of cocktails' Dale de Groff. Woody Allen and his jazz band perform most Monday evenings at the Carlyle, too.

ChamPino

1 measure Campari
1¼ measures sweet vermouth
Champagne, to top up

Pour the Campari and vermouth into a cocktail shaker and add some ice. Shake and strain into a chilled Martini glass. Top up with chilled Champagne and decorate with a lemon twist.

166 Milk and Honey *New York*

Sasha Petraske, the owner of this hip Lower East Side bar, caused a stir when he famously banned film auteur Quentin Tarantino from his establishment. In fact, anyone remotely famous is likely to be politely refused entrance. Admission is only for regular folks, albeit strictly by personal invitation; you must ring ahead in order to get through the heavily guarded door. Once inside, rules include: no raised voices, no exchanging of phone numbers, and gentlemen are forbidden from introducing themselves to ladies. For all that, Petraske mixes fantastic cocktails and has put together a list of twisted classics that is a masterpiece of modern mixology.

Bourbon Peach Smash

6 mint leaves

3 slices of peach

3 slices of lemon

2 teaspoons caster sugar

2 measures Bourbon

Muddle the mint, peach and lemon slices and sugar together in the bottom of a cocktail shaker. Add the Bourbon and some ice cubes. Shake and strain over crushed ice in a rocks glass. Decorate with a mint sprig and a lemon slice and serve with short straws.

Tonic *Boston*

Tonic is part sports bar and part dance club. Upstairs you can recuperate at the vast oval bar and watch the latest sporting action. Or head downstairs to the Met Lounge, a more intimate and music-oriented venue. Tonic has a long and inventive list of cocktails, along with a wide selection of draught beers and wines. Given the heavy Irish influence in Boston, it is hardly surprising that their signature cocktail is called the Celtic Six.

Celtic Six

½ **measure vodka**

½ **measure gin**

½ **measure white rum**

½ **measure silver tequila**

½ **measure Triple Sec**

½ **measure Midori**

dash of lime juice

lemonade, to top up

Pour all the ingredients, except the lemonade, into a cocktail shaker and add some ice. Shake and strain into an ice-filled sling glass. Top up with lemonade and decorate with slices of melon and lime and a cherry.

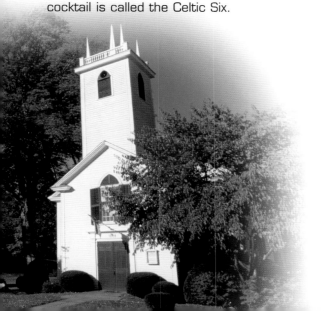

Green Mill Cocktail Lounge *Chicago*

A fixture of the Chicago lounge scene for almost 100 years, the Green Mill was a legendary gangster hang-out in the 1930s. During Prohibition, the bar was part-owned by mobster Jack 'Machine Gun' McGurn, one of Al Capone's henchmen. It has always been a fixture on the jazz circuit and has also served as a location for movies such as *The Untouchables* and *Prelude to a Kiss*. But it's not just showbiz here – the bartenders really know their stuff and turn out excellent Martinis and Manhattans along with the good stories.

Valentine Martini

2 measures raspberry vodka
6 raspberries
½ measure lime juice
dash of sugar syrup

Place all the ingredients in a cocktail shaker and add some ice cubes. Shake and double strain into a chilled Martini glass. Garnish with 2 raspberries on a swizzle stick, and a lime twist.

Zig Zag Café *Seattle*

Zig Zag is just beneath the famous Pike Place Market in downtown Seattle. Despite the hustle and bustle all around, the bar is a total retreat. Dimly lit and with plenty of bar seating and cosy sofas, it exudes a mellow calm. Legendary Seattle bartender Murray Stenson stocks the widest selection of spirits and liqueurs in town and takes his cocktail mixing very seriously. The classics are given the attention they deserve, but share menu space with some wonderfully original creations. The Aviation cocktail is made exceptionally well here, a rare find in most bars nowadays.

Aviation

2 measures gin
½ measure Maraschino liqueur
½ measure lemon juice

Pour all the ingredients into a cocktail shaker and add some ice cubes. Shake and double strain into a chilled Martini glass. Decorate with a cherry.

174 Tommy's *San Francisco*

This family-run establishment reputedly makes the best Margaritas in America. It also offers the largest selection of 100 per cent agave tequilas outside of Mexico: 225 at the last count. Julio Bermejo, son of the founder, runs the beverage side of the business; he ensures that each tequila is treated with the respect it deserves, adjusting his recipes depending on which brand is being used. For example, a Margarita using Herrudura Reposado will contain slightly less fresh lime than usual, whereas the recipe made with El Charro Anejo will highlight the intense vanilla qualities.

Margarita

1 lime wedge
rock salt
2 measures Herrudura Reposado tequila
1 measure lime juice
1 measure Triple Sec

Rub the rim of a coupette glass with the lime wedge, then dip it into rock salt. Pour the tequila, lime juice and Triple Sec into a cocktail shaker and add some ice cubes. Shake and strain into the salt-rimmed glass. Decorate with a wheel of lime.

Crush stocks over
40 different varieties of
Champagne and sparkling wine

CANADA

Crush Champagne Lounge *Vancouver*

Although it has only been open for business since 2002, Crush has already established itself as one of the hottest spots in the Vancouver social whirl. Part traditional lounge bar, part dance club, part live music venue, Crush has also become a popular venue for literary launches and fashion shows. The bar makes a great range of imaginative cocktails and stocks over 40 varieties of Champagne and sparkling wine, many served by the glass. These are enjoyed against a comfortable soundtrack of jazz, soul and local R&B.

Lush Crush

2 strawberries
dash of sugar syrup
2 lime wedges
1 measure Absolut Kurant vodka
Champagne, to top up

Muddle the strawberries, syrup and lime wedges in the bottom of a cocktail shaker. Add the vodka and some ice cubes. Shake and double strain into a chilled Champagne flute. Top up with Champagne and decorate with a sliced strawberry.

A GoGo Lounge *Montreal*

A wacky Quebec nightspot, A GoGo Lounge has a jazzy retro feel. The kitsch furnishings and psychedelic lighting might put one in mind of the Summer of Love, but the music is a mix of classic New Wave and Britpop. The dazzling array of Martini-style cocktails, using a fantastic selection of fresh fruit ingredients, are listed on menus made from old vinyl records and the pop-art feel is maintained with comic-book names such as Captain America and Kryptonite. The chosen cocktail was created for and enjoyed at Montreal's Fashion Week closing party.

Passion for Fashion

1½ measures golden rum

½ measure Grand Marnier

2 dashes of Angostura bitters

1 passion fruit

2 teaspoons passion fruit syrup

dash of lime juice

Place all the ingredients into a cocktail shaker and add some ice cubes. Shake and double strain into a chilled Martini glass. Decorate with cocktail cherries.

Beach Club *Las Vegas*

It may be miles from the nearest ocean, but that hasn't stopped Las Vegas establishing its very own Beach Club. Part of the Hard Rock Hotel complex, this hip nightspot offers a range of swimming pools, Jacuzzis and spa baths, private cabanas and a lagoon where the music plays underwater, not to mention two luxurious cocktail bars. You can order a drink at the swim-up bar and then try to win back what you have just spent by paddling over to one of the poolside gaming tables. Over the top and then some.

Hawaiian Deluxe

1½ measures coconut rum

½ measure Cointreau

½ measure aged rum

1 measure coconut cream

2 measures pineapple juice

dash of sugar syrup

dash of lemon juice

dash of grenadine

Pour all the ingredients, except the grenadine, into a cocktail shaker with some ice cubes. Shake and strain into a large hurricane glass. Drizzle the grenadine onto the drink before serving and decorate with pineapple and coconut wedges. Serve with long straws.

West *Toronto*

To find the West Lounge you have to cut down a back alley beyond the Cossette Building and look out for the luminous beacons that straddle the entrance. Once inside, you will find yourself surrounded by designer furniture, faux marble and opaque glass. Hardly surprising, then, to find that owner Marc Kyriacou was a former club designer of some note. Every cocktail under the sun is available in all three sections: the main bar, a hideaway with private booths and a VIP room.

Go West

½ **measure Frangelico**

1 **measure Limoncello**

1 **measure dry white wine**

½ **measure sugar syrup**

½ **measure lemon juice**

Pour all the ingredients into a cocktail shaker and add some ice cubes. Shake and double strain into a chilled Martini glass. Decorate with a lemon twist.

Marmont *Philadelphia*

Marmont is a lively and intimate lounge and a much-loved watering hole for Philadelphia's media types. Situated in the Old City district of Philadelphia and doubling as a steakhouse, Marmont offers a discreet, cosy space with lush furnishings and teardrop lighting. The innovative bar team experiments constantly with new ideas to produce a great new list of original cocktails every couple of months. The Fish House Punch has been synonymous with Philadelphia's drinking heritage since the 18th century and the recipe has remained largely unchanged.

Fish House Punch

1 measure brandy
1 measure golden rum
1 measure peach brandy
1 measure lemon juice
½ measure sugar syrup
1 measure cold tea (English Breakfast)
soda water, to top up

Pour all the ingredients into a cocktail shaker and add some ice cubes. Shake and double strain into an ice-filled highball glass. Top up with soda, decorate with a lemon wheel and serve with long straws.

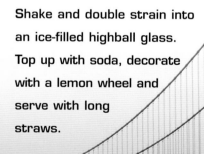

Tiki Bar *West Maui*

The Tiki craze dates back to the years following World War Two, when American servicemen returned from the South Pacific with recipes for such exotic cocktails as the Zombie and the Piña Colada. But for the authentic Tiki experience you need to head for Hawaii. The Tiki Bar on West Maui offers a relaxed setting during the day and an atmospheric night-time venue for live bands under a canopy of palm trees. Flamboyantly dressed bartenders relish the opportunity to impress with their latest creations – often blended into smoothie-style concoctions using seasonal fruit.

Tiki Treat

½ ripe mango, peeled and stoned

3 chunks of coconut

1 measure coconut cream

2 measures aged rum

dash of lemon juice

1 teaspoon caster sugar

Place all the ingredients into a blender and process with a small scoop of crushed ice until smooth. Serve in a stemmed hurricane glass with long straws and decorate with slices of ripe mango.

GLOSSARY

Bar syrup Used as a sweetening agent, bar syrup is an essential ingredient for any well-equipped bar. It is a mix of three parts sugar to one part water and comes in a variety of flavours.

Blend It is sometimes necessary to blend a cocktail which uses fresh fruit or crushed ice and this can be done by simply adding your ingredients to an electric blender or liquidizer, usually along with crushed or cracked ice, and blend for about ten seconds. Carbonated liquids should never be added to a blender as it is likely to cause the mixture to explode.

Build Simply fill your glass with ice, pour in the ingredients and serve.

Dash Ingredients with a very strong flavour, such as syrups and bitters, are usually added in very small quantities. A dash is literally a very small amount splashed into a drink.

Float This refers to a liquid or cream which forms a separate layer on top of another liquid. This can be achieved by gently pouring the liquid over the back of a spoon, making sure the spoon is touching the inside of the glass and is in contact with the drink.

Frappé A cocktail, liqueur or spirit poured over finely crushed ice and often served with a long straw so that the drink and the ice can be sipped together from the bottom of the glass.

Frosting A frosted glass has a coated rim, usually of sugar or salt. This can be achieved by wetting the rim of the glass with either water or egg white before dipping it in your chosen coating.

Muddle Fruit and herbs are often crushed in the bottom of a glass using a wooden pestle in order to release their juices and extract as much flavour as possible.

Neat A drink served without ice or a mixer.

On the rocks A drink served over a glassful of ice cubes. This serves to dilute the liquor slightly as well as chilling it.

Shake The technique it to put all the ingredients into a cocktail shaker along with cubed or cracked ice and shake vigorously using both hands until the outside of the shaker is frosty. The ice acts as a beater in the shaker as well as chilling the drink.

Spiral A strip of rind cut from a citrus fruit in a long spiral. This can be added to a drink for extra flavour or simply as decoration.

Stir Used for clear drinks whose appearance would be spoiled by vigorous shaking. Place the ingredients in a mixing glass and stir gently with a long-handled spoon before straining into a fresh glass.

Straight up A drink served without ice, usually in a tall glass.

Strain After a drink has been shaken or stirred, it is often necessary to strain the liquid into a glass to remove the ice or any fragments of fruit. This is done using a strainer. Some cocktail shakers come with their own strainer that fits over the shaker or mixing glass. Certain cocktails require double straining using a second strainer over the glass. This ensures a clearer liquid.

Swizzle stick This is a stirrer that is served with the drink. It acts as a decoration but can also be used to stir the drink when ingredients settle to the bottom of the glass.

Twist This is used as a garnish as well as to add extra flavour. It is made by cutting a long piece of peel, usually from a citrus fruit, and twisting it in the middle to release the oil from the outer zest.

Index

Acknowledgements

Author's Acknowledgements

Sarah, Alice, Geoff and Steve for loads of hard work.

All of the owners, bar managers, bartenders, PR crews and marketing departments, too numerous to name, who've willingly provided recipes and wisdom from their wonderful establishments.

Mum, Dad, Sarah, Richie, Jimi Mac, Ella, Eddie & Ernie, I love you all.

Paul, Guy, Jamie and Kylie – my precious roomies.

TC for offering your green sticks.

Muff, for the editorial advice and make-up tips.

Miss Shoo as always, miss you like crazy.

Al & Lisa, Doobs & Kez, Raff & Claire, Chet & Emma, Lasty & Iz, Murph & Vix, Jay & Marisa, Stu & Hoado – the happy couples X.

Publisher's Acknowledgements

Executive editor Sarah Ford
Editor Alice Tyler
Executive art editor Geoff Fennell
Designer Simon Wilder
Photographer Stephen Conroy
Drinks styling Allan Gage
Stylist Angela Swaffield
Picture researcher Jennifer Veall
Production Controller Ian Paton

The publisher would like to thank The Pier and Thomas Goode & Co. Ltd. for the loan of props.

Picture Acknowledgements:

Special Photography by Stephen Conroy

Alamy/Frank Chmura 62 /Keith Dannemiller 134 /Chad Ehlers 56 /Robert Harding World Imagery 70, 78 /Doug Pearson 147 /Carl Pedersen 69
Corbis UK Ltd 130 /Ricardo Azoury 124 /Dave Bartruff 48 /Tibor Bognar 97 /Marco Cristofori 36 /Derek Croucher 19 /Richard Cummins 20 /Macduff Everton 101 /Todd A. Gipstein 28 /Dallas and John Heaton 86 /Jon Hicks 31 /Dave G. Houser 155 /Karen Huntt 158 /Peter Johnson 74 /Ray Juno 111 /Catherine Karnow 82, 152 /First Light 178 /Gunter Marx Photography 177 /James Marshall 98 /Massimo Mastrorillo 32 /Buddy Mays 169 /John D. Norman 133 /Richard T. Nowitz 65 /Picimpact 35 /ML Sinibaldi 51 /Vince Streano 40 /Sygma 162 /Peter Turnley 52 /Michael S. Yamashita 93
Getty Images 44, 90 /Doug Armand 144 /Christopher Arnesen 116 /Jon Arnold 23 /Angelo Cavalli 143 /China Tourism Press 89 /Cosmo Condina 182 /Ron Dahlquist 119 /Jerry Driendl 185 /Chad Ehlers 59 /John Giustina 106 /Jorg Greuel 27 /Arnulf Husmo 55 /Adrian Lyon 173 /D. Noble 170 /Andrea Pistolesi 85 /Gary Randall 174 /Ken Ross 108 /B. Tanaka 181 /Joseph Van Os 73 /Simon Wilkinson 113 /Jeremy Woodhouse 123
Robert Harding Picture Library 14, 60, 77, 94, 102, 114, 120, 128, 137, 138, 140, 161 /C. Bowman 127 /N. Francis 156 /M. Mawson 148 /E. Rooney 166 /Omri Stephenson 80
Impact Photos /Philippe Achache 151 /Gold Collection 105 /Robin Laurance 47 /Alex Williams 186
Caroline Jones 24, 39, 43
Adam Monaghan 66
Rosewood Hotels & Resorts 165
Savoy Group Archives 16